COMPUTERS

**1988 Printing of the
1984 Revision**

BOY SCOUTS OF AMERICA
IRVING, TEXAS

Requirements

1. Do the following:
   a. Give a short history of computers. Describe the major parts of a computer system. Give four different uses of computers.
   b. Describe the differences between analog and digital computers. Tell the use of each.
   c. Explain some differences between special- and general-purpose machines.
2. Do the following:
   a. Tell what a program is and how it is developed.
   b. Describe a source program and an object program.
3. Discuss three programming languages and explain their major use(s).
4. Use a flowchart diagram to show the steps needed to set up a camp.
5. Do ONE of the following:
   a. Prepare flowcharts to find out the average attendance and dues paid at the past five troop meetings.
   b. Prepare flowcharts to work out a simple arithmetic problem. Explain to your counselor how this program could be stored in a computer. Tell how it could be used again.

Copyright 1984
Boy Scouts of America
Irving, Texas
ISBN 0-8395-3338-1
No. 3338   Printed in U.S.A.   20M188

6. Be prepared to discuss several terms in each of the following categories:
   a. Storage media
   b. Input/output devices
   c. Computer hardware
   d. Computer software
   e. Systems analysis and design
7. Visit a business or organization that uses a computer. Study how it works and be prepared to discuss what you have observed.
8. Describe several ways in which an individual or family can use a personal computer in the home other than for games.
9. Be prepared to discuss various jobs and careers in the computer field.
10. Write a computer program in any language to list the names and telephone numbers of the members of your troop. If you have access to a computer, execute the program. Review your program and the results of the program's execution (if available).

Contents

Introduction

The purpose of this *Computers* merit badge pamphlet is to give you a basic understanding of how people have developed ways to use computing machines to help them solve many problems. This pamphlet also should provide a starting point for in-depth study of computers, if you are interested.

This pamphlet describes computers and how they work, as well as many of the jobs people who work with computers do. Most of this pamphlet will focus on digital computers. When you have completed the requirements for this merit badge, you will know more about how computers affect our daily lives and about many jobs associated with computers.

What Is a Computer?

We must carefully distinguish between a computer and a calculating machine. In this pamphlet, we shall follow the definition of the word "computer" as given by the International Federation of Information

Processing and the American National Standard Institute: "*COMPUTER*—a data processor that can perform substantial computation, including numerous arithmetic or logic operations, without intervention by a human operator during the run." In this description, it is assumed that data processors are machines capable of working with data and include adding machines, slide rules, and even the abacus. A run is the sequence of operations that are necessary to find the solution to a problem. The feature that sets a computer apart from a calculating machine is the ability of the computer to perform without constant human intervention.

The computer is a tool that we use to help us perform a task. Just as an ax is an extension of our hand with which we can chop wood or a shovel is an extension of our arms with which we can dig a trench, the computer is an extension of our brain that can perform a great number of simple functions much faster than we can without becoming tired or bored. However, just like any other tool, the computer requires people—to write programs for it to perform. Some simple computers do not require programs because they can only do one task. Almost all the computers we will discuss in this pamphlet require a program written or developed by a person in order to perform a task.

There are two basic types of computers: digital and analog. *Digital computers* operate using numbers like the numerals displayed by a digital clock. *Analog computers* operate using measurements, such as how far something moves (the relative position of the hands of a clock as they move smoothly around the dial) or how much electrical current exists (the brightness of a light bulb or the loudness of a horn).

The Beginnings of Computers

A complete history of the development of computers would take a large book; we will just look at some interesting developments. The need to compute is as old as the human race. The computer today owes much to earlier inventions of calculating machines. Although the original purpose of computers was to provide a means for the fast solution of numerical problems, computers today are being used to provide solutions to many problems not directly related to mathematics or even to numbers. Computers have evolved from calculating machines that worked only with numbers. Obviously, an ox and cart is not in the same class as an automobile, but an automobile clearly is a descendant of the ox and cart, and both vehicles depended on the invention of the wheel. In the same way, the computer and calculating machine depended on the invention of mechanical methods to do arithmetic.

The abacus was developed in the Orient and was one of the early tools for working with numbers.

The Abacus

The first true calculating machine was the *abacus*, which is still used in some countries. It was in use before 400 B.C. and exists in three basic designs—the Chinese, the Japanese, and the Russian versions. Each style of abacus consists of a set of beads strung on wires within a rectangular frame. Each wire of an abacus represents a single digit in a number. The position of the beads on each wire represents a particular digit. In the Russian version, each wire holds 10 beads. In the Japanese

Figures of abacuses showing the number 629051

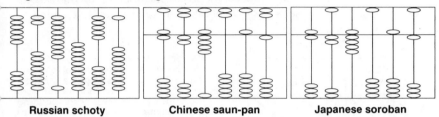

| Russian schoty | Chinese saun-pan | Japanese soroban |

and Chinese versions, each wire is divided into two fields, the upper part representing the number of fives and the lower part the remaining digits. In the Chinese version, the upper field contains two beads and the lower field contains five beads. In the Japanese version, the upper field contains one bead and the lower field contains four beads. With practice, it can be seen that the Japanese version is easier to use since there are fewer beads to move about and the number of beads in a group is easier to recognize by eye. A clever operator of an abacus can do arithmetic at amazing speed, easily as fast as a mechanical adding machine.

Napier's Bones

The problem of mechanizing the multiplication tables was solved in 1617 by a Scot, John Napier, who invented a set of rods on which were inscribed the multiplication tables. They were known as *Napier's bones* because the rods were made of ivory. Napier saw that the major problem in multiplication was to carry digits from one position to the next. His "bones" were so arranged that the units digit of one multiplication and the carry from the previous position were correctly seen. Although not really a mechanical device, Napier's invention led the way to later inventions of truly mechanical machines.

Napier also invented *logarithms*, which is a way to turn problems of multiplication and division into simple operations of addition and subtraction. The invention of logarithms led directly to the invention of the slide rule. A *slide rule* consists of two scales that can be moved against each other. A simple slide rule can be made with two pieces of cardboard marked off in equal intervals and numbered so that the scales match each other when the two cards are placed together. Addition can then be done by setting the zero position on the top scale opposite the first addend on the bottom scale. The result of the addition can be read on the bottom scale opposite the marker of the second addend on the top scale. (An addend is a number that is added to another in forming a sum.)

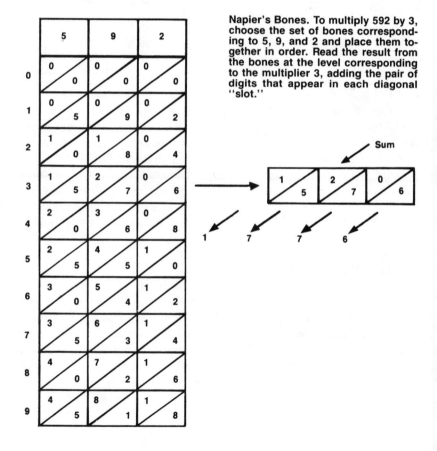

Napier's Bones. To multiply 592 by 3, choose the set of bones corresponding to 5, 9, and 2 and place them together in order. Read the result from the bones at the level corresponding to the multiplier 3, adding the pair of digits that appear in each diagonal "slot."

For addition:

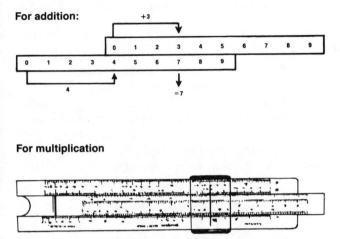

For multiplication

Adding Machine

The first real *adding machine* was invented by the French philosopher and mathematician Blaise Pascal in 1642. It worked much the same as modern desk adding machines. The digits from 0 to 9 were engraved on wheels. The first wheel represented 0 to 9; the second, the tens digit; the third, the hundreds digit; and so on, for eight columns. If the operator wanted to store (register) 136 in the machine, he would turn the third wheel to 1, the second to 3, and the first to 6. If he

Pascal's calculator

wanted to add 5 to this figure, he turned the first wheel five places. Through a series of gears, this action turned the second wheel from 3 to 4, for a total of 141.

Jacquard Loom

In 1801, a French weaver named Joseph M. Jacquard had an idea for automating a loom by using a punched board, the basis for the first modern computers. Making patterns in cloth was costly, and Jacquard got the idea of guiding the needles by allowing only the ones he wanted to use to go through the holes in a board. Very intricate patterns could be made cheaply by this early automatic loom, the *Jacquard loom*. The same principle was used in many early computers.

The Jacquard loom, developed for textile production, was operated by punched cards.

Hollerith Punched Card

Dr. Herman Hollerith, a statistician from Buffalo, New York, developed the *Hollerith punched card* and card machine, which was the first electrically driven computer. It was first used in the U.S. census of 1890. The method was to float each of the punched cards containing data

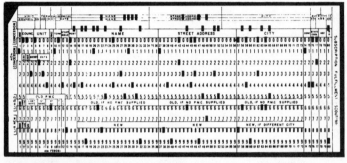

Hollerith punched card

about one American citizen across a pool of mercury. Telescoping pins overhead dropped through the holes. When a pin touched the mercury, it made an electrical contact, and one more fact about an American was recorded. To market his invention, Hollerith formed a company which, after a merger, became International Business Machines Corp. (IBM).

Electronic Computer

The first truly *electronic computer* was built at the University of Pennsylvania in 1946 by Dr. J. Presper Eckert and Dr. John Mauchly. The machine was named *ENIAC* (*E*lectronic *N*umerical *I*ntegrator and *C*omputer) and contained 18,000 vacuum tubes. Stories were told that when ENIAC was turned on, all the lights in a suburb of Philadelphia would dim! Parts of the ENIAC computer can be seen at the Smithsonian Institution.

During the period that ENIAC was developed, Dr. John von Neumann of Princeton University proposed a scheme for the control of computers by which the steps (called instructions) to solve a problem could be stored in the computer. This idea became known as the stored program concept. Computers that are designed on this basis are known as *stored program computers.* With this idea, the modern computer was truly invented. In fact, almost all digital computers today are basically the same as that described by Dr. von Neumann.

The first stored program computer in the United States was the *EDVAC* (*E*lectronic *D*iscrete *V*ariable *A*utomatic *C*omputer), also built at the University of Pennsylvania.

Later Developments

Although there has been little change in the basic design ideas of a computer since the EDVAC, the invention of transistors by Bell Telephone Laboratories in the early 1960s greatly increased the speed of computation and lowered the cost of production. The invention of the integrated circuit by Texas Instruments Corp. in the early 1970s lowered the cost even more. Today, computers are used for almost every conceivable application.

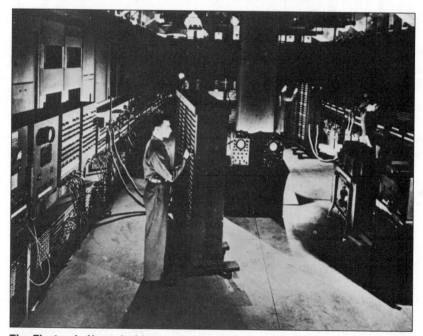

The Electronic Numerical Integrator and Calculator (ENIAC) was the first large-scale electronic computer. This machine was used by the Ballistic Research Laboratories of the U.S. Ordnance Corps. It weighed more than 30 tons and occupied more than 15,000 square feet. It had some 19,000 vacuum tubes and was able to perform 5,000 calculations a second.

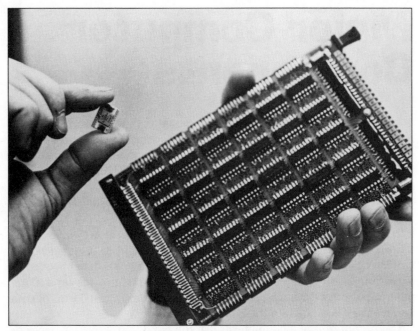

Advances in computer technology are highly visible in the comparison between the two computer logic units above. The circuitry at left can perform the same number of calculations as the circuitry at right. Since the invention of the integrated circuit, or chip, computers have become much smaller.

There are computers that fill large rooms and perform extremely complex tasks that would not have been possible a few years ago. There are minicomputers not much larger than a breadbox. Microcomputers are no larger than your thumbnail, and can be found in many everyday devices, including the telephone, television, automobile, wristwatch, and pocket calculator.

Major Computer Components

The components, or hardware, of a digital computer are best under-
stood if compared with the things a person does while solving a problem with pencil and paper. A computer has five major components: an
input unit, an output unit, a memory unit, an arithmetic unit, and a
control unit.

The *input unit* of a computer is like the eyes of a person who looks at
things around him (a book, a notepad) and transfers the data he sees
into his mind. The way an input unit reads data, however, is much
more elementary. For example, punched cards hold data encoded as a
pattern of holes punched in them. Magnetic tape holds data encoded as
an arrangement of magnetized spots on the surface of the tape. Computer input units (through special devices) can sense these forms of data
and transfer the data into the computer's memory.

The *output unit* of a computer is like the hand that writes on paper or
the mouth that speaks words. Data contained in the computer is trans-
ferred out of the computer by the output unit through special devices.
These devices either record the data on punched cards or magnetic
tape that computers can read or they write on television-like screens or
print on paper that humans can read.

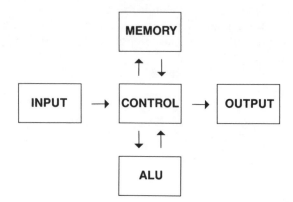

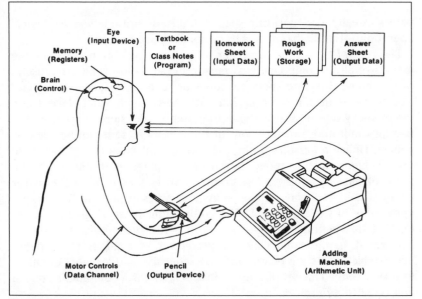

Comparison of the steps used by a person to solve a problem and the steps used by a computer to solve a problem.

The *memory unit* is like the recall process of a person who memorizes things that he may wish to refer to later. A computer's memory unit may store data in different ways using different kinds of storage devices. The devices vary in the amount of data they can store and the speed with which they can recall data that has been stored. The memory unit is different from a person's memory in two important ways: (1) the memory unit doesn't forget over time and, in fact, does not forget unless directly instructed to do so; and (2) the memory unit can store a definite limited amount of data and no more—to add some new data requires that some existing data be forgotten (erased).

The *arithmetic unit* of the computer performs calculations as a person performs calculations in his head. Just like you, most computers can perform basic arithmetic (addition, subtraction, multiplication, and division) with numbers. The arithmetic unit also can perform some *logical operations* such as "if this is true and that is true then..." Because the unit performs both arithmetical and logical operations it is sometimes called an *arithmetic logic unit* (ALU). Logical operations are somewhat like tiny decisions. Arithmetic units on special-purpose computers usually can perform special kinds of arithmetical or logical operations—that's what makes them special-purpose.

The *control unit* of the computer is like a person's brain, directing the actions of all its components. A person's brain controls all the muscles of the body, directing them to move or to be still. The control unit directs the input unit to bring data into the computer and place it into the memory unit. It directs the output unit to take stored data from the memory unit and transfer it out of the computer so it can be seen by people. Unlike a person's brain, the control unit knows only how to do simple things, such as move data from one place to another, or add a piece of data to another. The control unit is somewhat like a player piano, which can play all the individual notes of a song but has no knowledge of the song itself. The control unit must be given a set of explicit instructions that will result in some meaningful task when performed. In the same way, the player roll of a player piano determines which notes are played, in what sequence, and for what duration, to play a song. This set of explicit instructions for a computer's control unit is called a *program*.

Most digital computers in use today are made up of the five basic units described above. But there are many special-purpose computers used for special jobs. Some are faster than others in the way they transfer data or perform instructions while others have more memory capacity or input and output devices than others. In much the same way that special tools are used for particular jobs, special-purpose computers are used for special applications. *Application* is the term used most often when describing the "job" performed by a computer. It's the specific term for "what the computer is used for." In the next chapter, we'll look at some different computer applications.

The Uses of Computers

Computers are found at work in our society doing basically three types of jobs: scientific processing, information processing, and process control.

Scientific processing is the use of a computer to solve problems that are basically mathematical. Problems of this type would take many years for humans to solve working with pencil and paper, but can be performed in much less time by a computer.

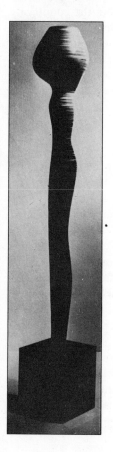

Information processing (or *business data processing*) is the use of a computer to handle large amounts of data—filing and keeping track of it so that it can be retrieved when needed. Used this way the computer becomes a fast file cabinet containing useful information. In fact, single computers are capable of storing as much information as a football field full of file cabinets. *Business data processing* is a form of information processing dealing with the management and control of business information, such as banking and inventory. The terms information processing and business data processing are often used interchangeably.

Process control is the use of a computer to monitor and control ongoing processes. Industries involved with constant processes, such as steel mills, electric power plants, and oil refineries, require constant monitoring of meters and gauges to ensure that everything is working properly. If something goes amiss, then something must be adjusted to make it right again. Jobs that require

Tranz computer sculpture in laminated veneer by Robert Mallary.

many people to sit and watch in case something needs to be adjusted can now be performed by process control computers. The computer can continuously monitor activities without getting tired. When the computer detects the need for an adjustment, it can call a person to make it or sometimes make the adjustment itself.

Of course, there are many variations on the three basic forms of computer applications. Let's look at a few specific applications of computers.

Internal Revenue Service

The Internal Revenue Service depends heavily upon computers to help it track all the tax information for the United States. Computer centers have been established in major cities throughout the country.

Tax return information for many years is filed by citizens' social security numbers. When a person files a return, a computer checks all entries for completeness and checks the taxpayer's arithmetic and deductions to make sure the tax is not higher or lower than it should be. If errors are found or if a person who has earned a salary does not file a return, the computer lets the IRS know about it.

Education

Computers are increasingly used in education. They are used in classrooms as teachers' aids and in principals' offices to keep records of students' grades and attendance and of budgets and salaries for the school's employees.

Teaching machines now offer programmed instruction *(computer aided instruction)* in which a student need almost never see a human teacher to complete a course. Both questions and answers are stored in the computer's memory. A student need only type an answer or make a choice in a multiple-choice quiz. The computer then checks the answer. If it is correct, the machine moves on to the next question. If it is wrong, the machine directs the student to where the solution can be found. In this way, a teaching machine can lead a student through a course, taking each area of learning step by step, and each student may proceed at his or her own pace. Simple computers have been used for many years to grade papers for multiple-choice quizzes.

Computers don't just help to teach students; computers can "learn" too. Programs have been written for computers to enable them to play tick-tack-toe, checkers, blackjack, Dungeons and Dragons, and chess. If

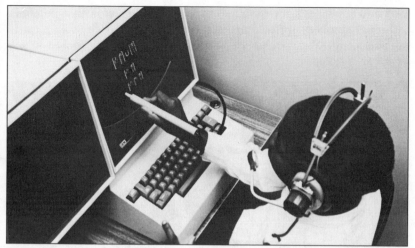
Computers are used to help students refine their skills in math and science. These instructional systems allow the student to work at his own speed.

a chess-playing computer makes a move during a game that leads to defeat, it will remember that move and avoid it in the future, learning by its mistakes. The computer does this by breaking down the problem into small steps, just as a human student handles a complicated mathematical problem.

So far, computers cannot match the best human chess players, but they offer a good challenge to most of us. Computers can be no better than the human who programs them to play the game.

Law

The number of legal documents in existence is so immense that no lawyer can possibly hope to examine them all without help; therefore, laws and court decisions have been classified and stored on computer. A lawyer simply gives the computer key words or phrases, and the computer searches its storage to respond with a list of cases and decisions that may pertain to the lawyer's question.

Computers also are used by law enforcement agencies to store and analyze the numbers and types of crimes committed in the country. With this information, agencies such as the FBI can decide the kinds of special crime-prevention training needed in particular areas of the country. Computers also help police find the owners of stolen property (cars and appliances, for example) by keeping track of license numbers and serial numbers of stolen articles. A common practice when a car is stopped for a traffic violation is to have a license plate checked to see if the car is stolen.

Computers are used to find fingerprints quickly.

Medicine

Computers are used in medicine for a variety of purposes. Some computers control delicate medical apparatus such as heart-lung machines or complex x-ray equipment. They are used to compile information on disease that may lead to new breakthroughs in medicine. Doctors have a catalog of more than 10,000 diseases they can check their diagnoses against.

Other computers, mostly the analog type, often are used to monitor the bodily functions of critically ill persons. Measuring

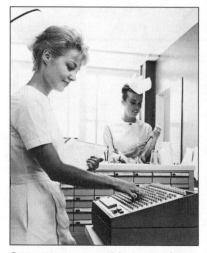

Computers are used in many phases of medicine.

devices are attached to the patient and connected directly to a computer that can keep a constant check of pulse, blood pressure, brain waves, and other vital functions. The slightest change in a patient's condition is detected immediately, often before there is any visual sign of change.

Computer terminals like the one shown at left are installed in many small hospitals and linked by telephone lines to the main computer. With this system, doctors in rural areas have access to the latest treatments for many diseases.

Transportation

Computers are used to test new ideas for the manufacture of cars, trains, planes, and boats. The ideas can be given to the computer, which then estimates how the ideas will work before any building has begun. This saves manufacturers time and money in finding out which ideas are useful and which ideas will probably never work. Computers can help plan highways and trip routes. They help transportation managers determine the best routes for their drivers to take and even advise

Computers are used to confirm airline reservations.

the managers of the number of vehicles they need to make the most profit. The superspeed trains common in Europe and Japan are controlled by computers.

Traffic Control

Most large airports now have computers to help air traffic controllers organize the takeoff, landing, and holding of aircraft in the area. At the same time, the computers are fed the routes, airspeed, estimated takeoff time, and other data from aircraft requesting approval of flight plans. Combining this information with weather forecasts, computers give pilots the best routes for their flights. Some aircraft have computers on board that communicate with computers on the ground, exchanging flight information much faster than humans could.

For automobile traffic, computers control traffic lights in cities. They can be programmed to change the timing of traffic lights depending on the volume or direction of traffic or at preset times. In large cities, where traffic congestion and parking are problems, computers are used to help people find suitable partners for car pools by matching their locations and work schedules.

Space

The U.S. space program owes much of its success to computers and the many people who use them. There could be no manned space flight program without computers. At every step in the preparation for a space launch and during the countdown and the flight itself, computers are busily making the instant calculations that are necessary. Computers are even used as simulators, allowing astronauts to practice piloting their spacecraft without leaving the ground. The computer controls meters and dials and can project pictures that make pilots feel as if they're actually flying the craft.

Weather Forecasting

The U.S. Weather Bureau and the Air Weather Service use computers in forecasting. Meteorological observations are taken hourly at stations all over the world. To keep forecasts up to the minute, the U.S. Weather Bureau relies on computers to analyze the great number of factors that must be considered in hourly forecasts. In fact, some of the larger and faster computers in use today were developed to support weather forecasting.

Telephone Switching

With the ever-increasing number of telephones being installed for both businesses and residences and the millions of calls being made locally and cross-country, the telephone companies have to rely on high-speed, electronic switching systems. These systems are computers developed by Bell Telephone Laboratories for this specific purpose. The computers keep track of the phone traffic and reroute long-distance calls depending on the load and the availability of circuits.

How Computers Differ

We can find out how the two types of computers differ by examining their names. The word "analog" is derived from the word "analogy," which means to make a comparison between things that are not similar in themselves. If you say, "A Scout is like a fencepost, straight and strong," you are making an analogy. Few Scouts look like fenceposts, but the analogy is true because most Scouts and fenceposts share the attributes of being straight and strong.

The word "digital" comes from the Latin word "digitus," meaning finger or toe. It still means finger or toe to zoologists. In mathematics, it means a figure from 0 to 9.

The words "analog" and "digital" suggest the basic difference between the two types of computers: an analog computer compares two things and gives an approximate measurement; a digital computer counts figures and gives an exact total.

Simple Analog Devices

One of the most familiar analog devices is the speedometer in your family car. As the car's wheels rotate, a message is sent to a device under the dashboard. This device transforms the message into a reading on a dial. It is an approximation only, and its accuracy depends on how good the speedometer is. If the dial reads 50 miles an hour, the car may actually be traveling 48 or 52 miles an hour, but a good speedometer gives a close approximation. Thermometers and bathroom scales are other common examples of analog devices.

Speedometer

24

Simple Digital Devices

The first digital computer was the abacus. All digital computers deal directly with digits or numerals, not with quantities or other measurements.

Modern Analog Computers

Since digital computers are more accurate than analogs, why bother with analogs at all? Why not use only digital computers?

In fact, digital computers are gradually supplanting analogs in most fields, but analogs still have their uses because they have certain advantages. Analogs usually are simple. Consider the thermometer. A digital computer could be built that would record temperatures, but it would not likely be as simple. Another advantage of analogs is speed—the analog measures the operation as it happens.

Not all analogs are simple devices such as speedometers, slide rules, and thermometers. There are complex analogs, almost comparable in complexity to their digital cousins.

Many complicated analog computers are used in aircraft design, in controlling the flow of electric power, in controlling automatic machine processes, and in other applications where simultaneous monitoring of the work is necessary. Analogs also are useful in chemical and petroleum refineries, where each step of the work must be under constant control.

Analog computers have the advantages of simplicity and speed in certain applications. They are, however, less accurate than digital computers, and most analogs are specialists—they do only one job.

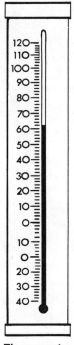

Thermometer

Modern Digital Computers

The digital computer has no intelligence. About the most complex thing it knows how to do is add 1 and 1. All of its mathematical genius is really just being able to repeat the addition of two digits over and over again. But it is capable of millions of such operations a second.

Digital computers are constantly adapted to new uses because of these advantages over the analog computer:

• Greater accuracy.
• More flexibility.
• More compactness.
• They can handle problems of logic that are beyond the analog.

The digital computer suffers in comparison with the analog only for some purposes—the analog computer will give an immediate answer to a problem that the digital computer will answer in a second or two.

Boy Scouts learn some of the uses of modern digital computers.

Special-Purpose and General-Purpose Machines

Computers can be classified by the tasks they are designed to perform. Large *general-purpose machines* in service centers must be capable of performing the many different tasks required by the center's clients. Such machines often are much larger than is necessary to solve any particular problem, and thus much more expensive than a machine designed for one specific purpose. The availability of microcomputers at a low cost permits the exclusive use of a single computer for a single task.

A general-purpose home computer

Where a computer will be asked to solve one special type of problem, it may be better to design a computer for that one task than to use a machine that was designed to solve all kinds of problems. The computers that "fly" with the astronauts are *special-purpose machines* and are efficient at their particular task, but they may be totally useless for anything else, such as playing chess.

The ancient Britons built a special "computer" to predict the times of the eclipses. This computer we know as Stonehenge, and it obviously is not much use for computational purposes other than predicting the occurrence of seasonal events. Given sufficient time and energy, a human using an abacus could have solved the same problem Stonehenge was built to solve. Many analog computers are special-purpose machines, and some digital computers—which are designed as general-purpose systems—become special-purpose when they are tied in to other equipment. For example, in hospitals a general-purpose computer can be attached to monitoring devices to watch over the vital signs of a patient. In this use, these machines cannot (dare not) be used for any other purpose and, thus, become special-purpose.

Many companies now sell personal computers for home use. Usually these use a microcomputer and are general-purpose.

Computer Programs

The parts of a computer that can be touched and seen usually are referred to as *computer hardware* because they are hard. The programs that control the operations of that hardware usually are called *computer software* because, unlike the hardware, programs can't be seen or touched once they're inside the computer's memory.

To use a computer to solve problems, a person must prepare in advance a detailed set of instructions for the computer to follow. The set of instructions, the program, must be complete in every way. The program must describe in exact detail the steps to be performed and the actions to be taken when particular situations arise. The computer is so senseless that it can't guess; unlike a human being, a computer has no

A Boy Scout receives instructions for using a general-purpose home computer.

imagination. Every possibility must be taken into account by the person writing a program so that the machine always knows what to do next. A computer does not understand the statement "You know what I mean." Once you have programmed a problem and executed it, the computer has to be told again the next time the same type problem is to be solved.

Computers basically can do only simple arithmetic with the numbers 1 and 0 (*binary* arithmetic). Therefore, if we write instructions in a form that a computer can directly use, it will have to be in the form of many 1's and 0's. That language has an "alphabet" of only 1 and 0. Like the Morse code, a language with an alphabet of dots and dashes, the particular patterns of 1's and 0's have particular meanings to the computer. Not only would writing programs this way be tedious and boring, it also would be prone to error because even simple programs require thousands of 1's and 0's.

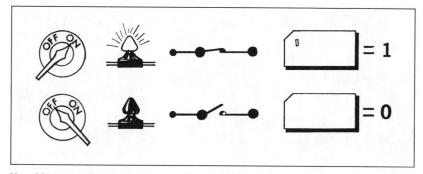

How binary numbers are expressed electrically

To get around this problem, computers usually come equipped with *translators* that can take programs written in a language that is easier for people to work with and produce a program of 1's and 0's that the computer can execute directly. Like human translators who translate from one language into another, a computer translator translates from a human-like language into the computer's language.

A program is developed in four stages:

- A description of the problem, usually written in English, may be provided by the person wanting the problem solved explaining how he would go about solving the problem if he had to do it by hand.

- A description of how the computer would solve the same problem usually takes the form of a diagram (often a flowchart) that identifies each step to be taken in the solution of the problem and the decisions to be made at each step.
- The writing of the program, usually in special human-like language *(programming language)*, is then sent to the computer for translation into computer language.
- The program is finally tested using output data that should produce certain results. If the expected results are produced, the program is ready for use.

A program (which is not tiny) rarely works the first time because there are so many instructions and the possibility of human error is always high (even in just typing the program). The process of correcting the program is known as *debugging* (getting the flaws out).

Binary digits, the computer's language

Assembler and Compiler

Programming languages have been invented to help programmers express the solution to their problem in a convenient manner. Unlike early programmers, today's programmers do not have to be computer hardware experts. Modern programming languages offer a programmer a dialect that is independent of the particular hardware.

The historical development of programming languages may be traced in three steps. Originally, a programmer had to understand the electronic workings of a computer in order to design a program that would solve a problem. A program was written in *machine language,* which consisted of 1's and 0's (known as *bits,* a term derived from *binary digits*) that had to be placed in the memory of the machine at the correct locations. This was extremely tedious. Although many aids were constructed to help, a programmer had to know everything about how the computer worked to perform a task.

At the next step, a set of statements was written in English-like language, each describing a single step in the solution of the problem. These statements were then translated into the actual language of the computer (machine language). This new language was known as *assembly language,* because the program to translate it assembled machine language. This was a vast improvement over writing programs in machine language. Now the programmer could write commands such as "add" (for add) or "div" (for divide) instead of having to remember the binary code in machine language for those instructions. The translator of an assembly language is known as an *assembler.*

As machine designs improved, each type of design came to have its own machine language and, hence, its own assembly language. Thus, a program written for one machine could not be used on another machine of a different type. To overcome this problem, languages were invented that were more "machine independent." These early languages were somewhat more "human" than assembly languages, but they referred to mathematical problems rather than everyday problems. In this style of language, a mathematical expression can be written in a form such as $D = A + B$ instead of the assembly language sentence (to be taken in order) get A; add B; store in D. The program that translates higher level languages into machine language is known as a *compiler.*

The program written by a programmer to express the instructions for solving a problem is known as the *source program;* the program that results from translation either by an assembler or by a compiler is known as an *object program.*

Programming Languages

Programming languages, like computers, can be classified as general-purpose and special-purpose. Many languages are general-purpose and are designed to assist in the description of many types of computer-related problems. Specialized programming languages have been developed to help program particular problems, for engineers and surveyors, for example. These languages are not generally suited for use other than that for which they were specifically designed. They are particularly well suited to let engineers or surveyors express the solution to a problem in terms they are familiar with.

Today, we consider most assembly languages to be special-purpose since they can only be used to write programs for a particular machine. Translators, for example, are programs themselves often written in assembly language. Assembly languages are used as special-purpose languages to write programs that provide the tools to solve problems (software tools) rather than solving problems themselves. Software tools can be compared to machinists' tools that make hammers and saws, which are then used in other tasks.

Two general-purpose languages are commonly used for writing programs: *FORTRAN* (*for*mula *trans*lation) and *COBOL* (*com*mon *b*usiness *o*riented *l*anguage). Perhaps 80 percent of all industrial programming uses these languages. FORTRAN is widely used for the writing of scientific programs by scientists and engineers, primarily to manipulate mathematical computations. COBOL is designed to perform business-related functions such as record keeping, accounting, and storing large volumes of written information.

Several other general-purpose languages also are found, but not nearly so often: *ALGOL* (*algo*rithmic *l*anguage), *PL/1* (*p*rogramming *l*anguage *1*), and *Pascal.* These languages have developed as prospective replacements for assembly language in the writing of software tools. *BASIC* (*b*eginners *a*ll-purpose *s*ymbolic *i*nstruction *c*ode) is a language that has become popular for writing programs for microcomputers (especially personal computers) because it is easily learned and allows most simple programming tasks to be accomplished without much professional knowledge.

Special-purpose languages are not generally known by most programmers. They usually are familiar to programmers who often write programs to solve particular kinds of problems. A few special-purpose programming languages are COGO (*co*ordinate *g*eometry), used by civil engineers; ECAP (*e*lectronic *c*ircuit *a*nalysis *p*rogram), used by electrical engineers; LISP (*lis*t *p*rocessing language), used by language researchers in artificial intelligence applications; STRESS (*str*uctural *e*ngineering *s*ystems *s*olver), used by mechanical engineers; and TUTOR, a language for preparing computer-assisted instruction courses under the PLATO system. There are almost as many special-purpose languages as there are applications.

Flowcharts

One way to show the workings of a program is to draw a picture that shows the sequence of actions and decisions that the program will perform. A picture of this kind is often called a *flowchart.* Before

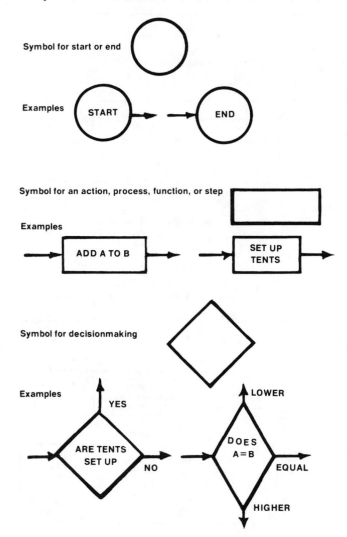

A simple flowchart

Flowchart for Computers Merit Badge

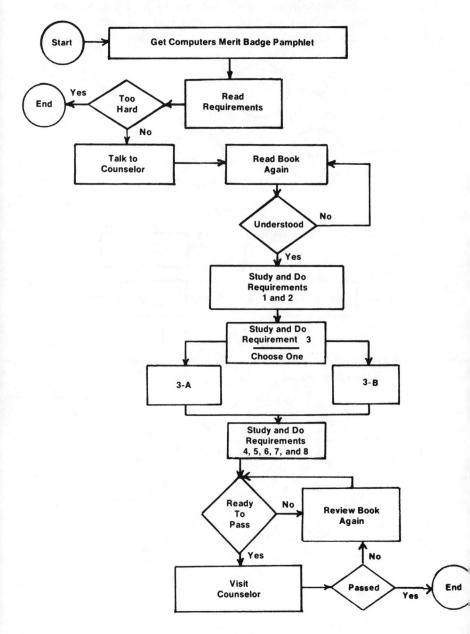

programming, a programmer will make a flow diagram or flowchart of the logic required to solve a problem. This helps ensure the programmer that the program will perform the proper steps. A flowchart also breaks down the problem into groups of simple steps (building blocks), just as you would break down a problem to solve it in your head. This allows the programmer to concentrate on each small, manageable block, one block at a time, and to later arrange the blocks properly to build the completed program.

A flowchart is a picture or diagram of the steps required to solve a problem, presented by a few simple geometric symbols.

Campsite Setup

Setting up a campsite is not an arithmetic problem, it is a logic problem. Your flowchart for requirement 4 will have directions, questions, and answers rather than digits.

Keep in mind that many steps may seem self-evident to you, but they would not be to a computer. Remember that the computer is dumb, and it "knows" only what you put into the logic of your flowchart. You must consider every move and every question that goes into establishing a campsite.

Here are several steps that should be included:

Step 1. Choose site for patrol camping. Specify reasons for choosing site. Have patrol unpack gear and set up tents.

Step 2. Patrol leader designates chores to do before anyone can eat:
Fetch wood.
Build fire site.
Fetch water for fire buckets.
Cooks prepare meals.
Start fire and cook food.
Have remaining Scouts clean up area and set up eating area.

Step 3. Food is divided up and all eat.

Step 4. Divide patrol into buddies.

Step 5. Dig latrine, if needed.

Step 6. Buddies clean up dishes, gather more firewood, and get drinking water.

Step 7. When all is completed, plan other activities for remainder of campout.

Organizing a Program

A simple way to think about writing programs is to consider the pocket calculator, which is a little brother of the computer. A calculator can perform a few important functions called *operations,* for which there are keys on the calculator. The operations may be performed in any order that the user of the calculator wishes. Not all sequences of key presses will result in meaningful calculations; only certain sequences are useful. But there are many useful sequences. When you develop a sequence of key presses to perform some task on a calculator, you actually are developing a program of steps to solve a particular problem. This is the equivalent of writing a program for a large general-purpose computer. But, instead of your having to remember the sequence of operations in your head or on paper, you can have the computer remember the sequence for you and have it perform that sequence as often as you wish.

A program is made up of a set of individual instructions. These *instructions* are the detailed steps to be taken to solve a particular problem. The different types of instructions, such as add or divide, are limited to a small number in each machine. The number of different possible actions that can be done by a machine is fixed by the manufacturer. It is the programmer's job to use this small set of instructions to make a program that will solve a complex problem. Large computers may accept as many as 200 different instructions.

When the program is to work on data organized by the programmer as a table or list, it is often necessary for the computer to work with entries in the table or list in turn. For example, you may have been given a homework problem that said, "Answer the following set of questions." You would complete your assignment by answering each question in turn. The process of selecting each element of a set, table, or list in order is called *indexing.* Some computers provide special registers (index registers) in the central processing unit that help a programmer keep track of which element of a table or list the program is to work on next.

We are often given an assignment to answer a set of questions, each really the same problem with different values. If a program can be written that solves one of the problems, it could be able to solve the others in the same way. In fact, that is what the computer is good at doing—solving the same type of problem over and over. If you were given 20 problems to solve, you might do well on the first few, but then you might start getting tired or bored and start making mistakes. The computer doesn't get tired or bored and is good at doing the same problem over and over again.

If a program had to be written every time a problem was to be solved, a programmer might as well solve the problem by hand, because it often takes as long, or longer, to write a program as it does to solve a problem. Only when the same program can be used many times does the program pay for itself. Some problems are solved by doing the same work over and over again (a process called *iteration*) until a complete solution is reached. A computer program written so that one group of instructions is used over and over again to solve the same problem with different data is called a controlled *loop*.

It would be a tremendous waste of time and effort to write a program, use it once, and then throw it away. Therefore, programs are stored on drums, disks, or tape for use at another time. If a program has already been written to solve a problem, it would be unfortunate if it were not available to everybody who had the same type of problem to solve. Libraries are therefore developed on drums, disk, or tape from which programmers can borrow programs. In many cases, a programmer will write a program that includes another program from the library. The programmer will borrow the program in the library by copying it into the larger program. This borrowed program is known as a subprogram or *subroutine*. Most libraries have subroutines available for calculating trigonometric functions (sine, cosine, tangent), square roots, and logarithms; sorting a list of numbers; and many other jobs.

Types of Storage

So far, we've concentrated on what happens inside the computer—how it computes things. Another important part of computers is how they store data outside themselves for later use.

Every computer has a memory like your own that can recall immediate facts; we usually call this *primary storage*. Unlike humans, whose memory isn't lost after sleep, most computers' memory is lost when they are turned off. Also, most computers have a limited primary storage capacity (less than a hundred library books' worth). When they finish one problem and move to the next, some of their storage must be erased (old information forgotten) to make room for the next problem.

This capacity problem is solved much like humans solve the need for more information than we can remember in our heads. Much like a library, most computers have access to storage that retains the information stored in it even when it's turned off. This storage is often called

These Boy Scouts are looking at a disk pack that has been cut away to show the platters on which the data is stored.

secondary storage. Secondary storage is like a library filled with books. The computer can call up one book at a time to retrieve particular information. Just as in libraries, some books can be found quickly because they are stored in special ways, and others take longer to locate and retrieve.

Let us examine some devices for building a storage system. Four basic types of storage are commonly used: metal oxide semiconductor (MOS), magnetic drum, magnetic disk, and magnetic tape. Each of these storage devices is both an input and an output device, receiving, storing, and retrieving information.

All four devices are designed to use the principles of electromagnetism— the laws that govern electricity and magnetics. If you get lost on a hike, you can pull out your compass and find north because the needle is attracted to the magnetic north pole. It it were possible to switch the earth's north and south poles, the compass needle would reverse itself and point in the opposite direction. Although this can't be done, it is possible to reverse a magnetic field electrically. This property of electromagnetism is used to give memory to a digital computer.

MOS

The most widely used type of memory device is the MOS, *m*etal *o*xide *s*emiconductor, because it stores great amounts of information in a small space and because each bit of information is easy to find. The physics of how MOS actually works is somewhat complicated, so we'll use an analogy to describe it.

Let's assume that each 1 or 0 is stored in the memory as a tiny magnet that points either north or south, and that we can make it swap directions by sending an electrical current through that magnet. Let's

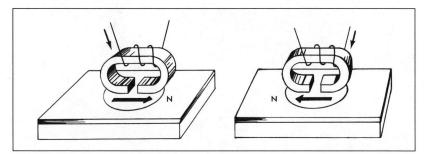

A magnetic field can be changed electrically.

assume the current is carried by wires that run through a hole in each magnet (like a doughnut). We'll call each of the magnets a magnetic core.

Magnetic cores are tiny, doughnut-shaped rings of iron-containing (ferrite) material a few hundredths of an inch in diameter. They look like the small beads you would use for an Indian belt or headband. More than a million cores are used in large computers. They are woven together somewhat as you would weave Indian beads, but several wires run through each core. Each core is magnetized in either a clockwise or counterclockwise direction, and the direction of its magnetism represents one bit of information for the computer (either 1 or 0, yes or no, for example).

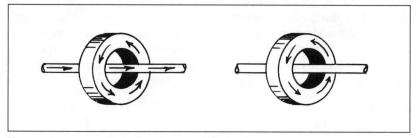

Memory cores are magnetized to store information.

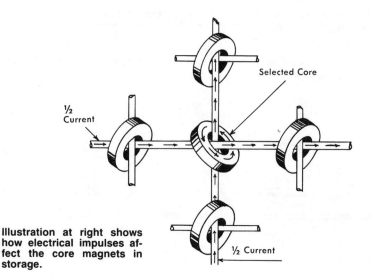

Illustration at right shows how electrical impulses affect the core magnets in storage.

When the proper pulse of electrical current is sent on a wire through one of these ferrite cores, the core reverses its magnetic field (1 becomes 0, 0 becomes 1). The computer can store information in one of a million cores by dividing the electrical current needed to reverse its magnetic field and sending half of it through the proper vertical wire and half through the horizontal wire. Suppose we want to store 1 or 0 in the core at the intersection of vertical wire 71 and horizontal wire 37. Half the current needed is sent through wire 71 and half through wire 37.

Information that has been stored in the core storage is read by sensor wires interlacing all the cores. These wires communicate to the computer the status of each core (whether it is in the 0 state or the 1 state). The process is more complicated than it sounds, but it is still an instantaneous reading. The assembly of wires and cores is called a *core storage plane.*

You can build a simple model of a core storage plane to explain how it works by stringing beads or washers on wires attached to a wooden frame. This will be a nonworking model, of course, but it will help you picture core storage operation.

Rotating Storage Devices

If we put a tiny spot of magnetic material on any surface, it will act like a magnet. If it is placed in a strong magnetic field, it will align itself with that field. If we change the direction of the field by using an

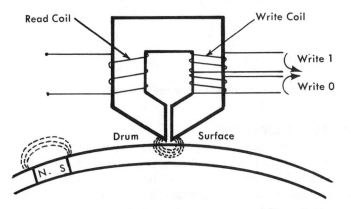

Magnetic "read-write" head, *above,* **stores information on the drum and "reads" it on command of the machine.**

electromagnet, the tiny magnetic spot will change its direction, too. The direction of this spot, then, can represent one bit of information for a computer.

To see how this works, let's move our magnetized spot past the ends of a U-shaped iron core with a coil of wire attached. Since the spot acts like a permanent magnet, it has a small magnetic field of its own. By moving the magnetized spot through the same electromagnet with which we magnetized it, we create a current in the electromagnet. The direction of this current depends on the direction in which the magnetic spot was aligned. Therefore, the computer can tell whether the spot represents a 1 or a 0.

The computer can read, write, or erase (by writing 0's) one bit of information on each spot of magnetic material. On drum, disk, or tape storage devices, the electromagnet that does the reading, writing, and erasing is called a *read-write head.*

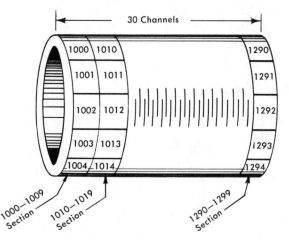

Bits of information are organized for storage on a magnetic drum.

Magnetic Drums

Magnetic drums are rotating metal cylinders marked with parallel bands or *tracks.* Each track may be spot magnetized in either direction by an electrical impulse. A read-write head above each track serves as a recorder and sensor. Magnetization in one direction will represent a 1, while in the other direction it will mean a 0.

Magnetic Disks

Magnetic disks operate the same way as drums. They look like phonograph records and rotate in the same way. Rigid disks are made of

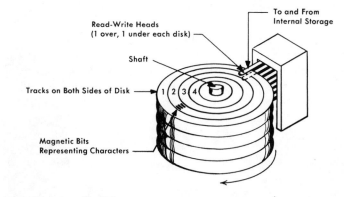

Read-Write Heads
(1 over, 1 under each disk)

To and From
Internal Storage

Shaft

Tracks on Both Sides of Disk

1 2 3 4

Magnetic Bits
Representing Characters

Diagram of a magnetic disk

metal, and their surfaces can be spot-magnetized like the tracks on the magnetic drum. Several read-write heads may be positioned along the disk so that data can be read and recorded quickly. Flexible disks, sometimes called *diskettes* or *floppy disks,* are made of mylar with surfaces that can be spot-magnetized. Mylar is the same material used for making cassette recording tapes; it is strong and flexible. Diskettes are sealed in a lubricated sleeve and have two recording surfaces, much like a 45 rpm record.

Some magnetic disks have an advantage over both drums and metal oxide memories: they can be removed from the cabinet and replaced like phonograph records. Information can be stored on the disk for use at a later date, and the disks can be put into a "library." Disks can be labeled by the operators and filed away until the next time the computer needs that particular information. For example, if a company only runs its payroll calculations once a month, there is no need to have employees' salary rates information available all the time. Only when there are changes in employees, when someone gets a salary raise, or when the payroll checks are to be produced is that particular disk needed in the computer system. The rest of the time, when the computer is doing other tasks, other disks can be installed, thus expanding the effective storage capacity of the computer.

Magnetic Tape

The material used in *magnetic tape* units is flexible but otherwise acts like the material used to build drums or disks. The tape is much like that used in your home or school tape recorder, though it is wider (usually ½ inch) and moves much faster past the read-write heads. Magnetic tape is wound onto reels, each reel containing as much as 2,400 feet of tape. Since 1,600 (or as many as 6,250) characters can be stored on 1 inch of tape, it is theoretically possible to have as many as 46 million characters on a tape. That number is reduced considerably since gaps must be left at the beginning and end of the tape to allow it

These Boy Scouts are looking at a tape drive, which reads and writes data on a magnetic tape.

to be fixed onto the reels and fed through the machine, and between recordings so that it can stop before the next recording is read.

Like disks, reels of tape can be removed from the computer, providing enormous storage capabilities. Many computing centers have magnetic tape libraries.

Organization of a Storage System

The cost of providing storage in a computer is the price of the equipment divided by the amount of storage provided. The units of measurement are usually cents per bit. In order of decreasing cost, the storage devices are MOS, drum, disk, and magnetic tape. This order is exactly the same if the list is arranged from fastest to slowest in providing access to the information stored in the devices.

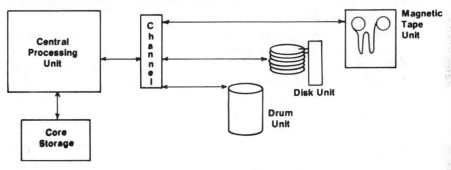

A multilevel storage scheme

Speed is measured as the time it takes the central processing unit to begin receiving information from a storage device after information has been requested. This delay occurs because of several factors. In the MOS, the circuits must be set up to select a particular bit. In the drum and on the disk the read heads are fixed in position; the computer must wait for the device to rotate until the recording needed is under the read head. The read heads must be moved vertically on the disk to select the particular disk in the set and moved horizontally to the position of the information on the disk (called the track). When using a magnetic tape, the heads remain in one position and tape must be moved past them to get to the information. When using both removable disks and tapes, the required device may not be on the system, so the computer must wait until the operator has installed the proper device.

Every attempt is made to get the best use out of the cost of the memory devices on the system. The most frequently needed information is stored on the devices that can retrieve it the fastest; the least frequently needed information is stored on the devices that take longer to retrieve it. This is similar to the way you would pack a backpack. Those things you might need in a hurry are packed where you can get to them quickly and those things of less urgency are packed in the bottom of the pack.

Based on the cost of the devices and the time it takes to get the information, the following is a likely scheme for the storage of different types of information:

- MOS storage—programs and data actually in use.
- Drum storage—permanent programs (including compilers and assemblers) that are used very often.
- Disk storage—programs and data used regularly but which are not always necessary for the operation of the computer system.
- Magnetic tape—infrequently used programs and data or new programs and data that are being given to the system for the first time. Also used for permanent copies of the programs and data stored on the disk or drum in case anything goes wrong.

The technology of storage media is ever-changing. Recently, storage devices that store 1's and 0's as bubbles of magnetism have been introduced and are called *bubble memory.* Lasers are being tested that can imprint a million dots of information by burning tiny holes in an area the size of the head of a pin. This form of storage can be written only once but may be read as often as required. Much information is written once and read many times—books, catalogs, maps, and video discs for example. Most of the changes in storage technology have to do with storing more information in smaller and smaller spaces. We can expect these kinds of changes to occur continually. Regardless of the technology, the new memories will probably behave much like the four types we have described.

Input/Output Systems

The three communications systems we shall consider are the printed word (numbers and words in a written language), pictures (words and numbers represented by diagrams), and sounds (words and numbers in an audible language). Each of these communications systems can be used either to transmit information to a computer or to transmit results from a computer.

Printed Word

The simplest form of input/output system connected to a computer uses the printed word. As far back as the Jacquard loom, the communication of information to a computer has taken the form of the written word. Unfortunately, the technology by which a computer can "read" a page of writing or printing is not always the most efficient means of

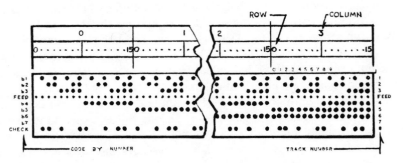

Punched paper tape

information transfer for machines. We have been compelled to use communications systems more closely geared to the computer than to our own methods of communication. Thus, the "printed word" for input to a computer often takes the form of holes punched in paper.

Two standard forms of punched input were once common: the *punched card* and the *punched paper tape*. Each form has characters (letters,

The printer these Boy Scouts are watching can print addresses on 45,000 *Boys' Life* mailing labels in less than an hour.

numbers, and some special characters such as period, comma, and semicolon) represented as holes whose codes the machine can recognize. The original data processing card, designed by Dr. Herman Hollerith, was the same size as the 1890 dollar bill. The horizontal dimension of a card represents the message to be transmitted, with each vertical column representing an individual character. The number of holes and their position in each vertical column is the coding for a character.

A card can contain only a certain amount of information because it has a fixed length, but a tape can be as long as the programmer needs. Tape is usually made of paper, although mylar plastic and foil have been used. The length represents the message, and the width contains the punched code for individual characters of the message.

The devices to read cards or tapes can be either electromechanical or photosensitive. The simplest form is the electromechanical system, in which the holes and their positions are determined by metal "feelers." When these feelers drop through a hole they complete an electrical circuit and send a signal to the computer.

In a photosensitive reader, the card or tape is passed under a light source and over a set of photoelectric cells. When the light passes through a hole, the photocells react and send a signal to the computer.

Computers have printing devices that convert signals into printing on paper. The simplest form of *printer* is the teletype, which is like a special form of typewriter. In this device the electrical signals from the computer turn a cylinder to face the paper, print the character, and then move to the next position on the paper.

This kind of printing device is slow compared with the speed of the computer in getting answers. High-speed printers have been developed that are capable of printing a whole line at one time or even a whole page at one time. Like the teletype, the line printer has all the characters that are possible to be printed etched on chains, wheels, or cylinders. As the signals arrive from the computer, each wheel in the line is set to the required character. When the whole line is set up the line is printed on the paper. Some high-speed printers are not mechanical; they print by burning or spraying ink on the paper. Others use special photographic paper and a high-intensity light to create images of the characters on the paper, which is later developed.

Words on a page also can be input to a computer through a device known as an *OCR* (*O*ptical *C*haracter *R*ecognizer). This device can actually read a page and tell the central processing unit what it saw. In some devices, special printing is required on the page to help the reader interpret the message. In common use today are the magnetic ink characters on bank checks, which can be read by a human and by a machine.

Diagrams and Drawings

The second type of input/output system, called a *plotter,* uses diagrams or drawings to communicate.

One kind of plotter consists simply of a sheet of paper on a movable drum that the computer draws on with a pen. The drum can move the paper forward or backward, and the pen can be moved sideways and lifted off the paper. By moving the drum and pen together, the plotter can draw lines at almost any angle. By careful programming, the computer can make engineering drawings and even produce works of art.

A television-like device also can be attached to a computer. The device, often used by engineers and physicists, is known as a *CRT* (*C*athode *R*ay *T*ube). In a CRT, an electron beam can be controlled to light up the face of the tube in the same way the pen was controlled on the plotter. However, the electron beam can be moved much faster; pictures or diagrams can be produced in fractions of a second. If produced fast enough, the pictures appear to move, as if on television. The CRT can be used by cartoonists and animators to produce movies.

Both the CRT and the plotter are output devices, but the CRT may also be an input device. Using photoelectric cells, a special *light pen* was developed that is capable of detecting light on a CRT. Using a CRT,

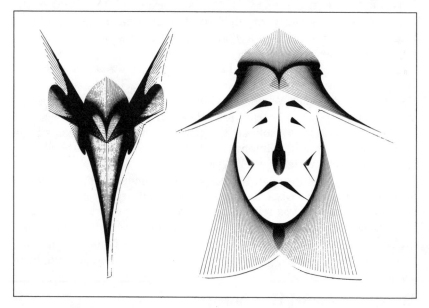

"Hummingbird," *left,* and "The Fisherman," computer art produced by California Computer Products, Inc.

With an electronic light pen, a user can revise diagrams and through the keyboard change information and images on the screen. This was developed for scientists and engineers who need fingertip access to a computer.

a special program, and a light pen, a computer user can "draw" on the CRT screen and give a problem to the computer in graphic terms rather than in writing. Other CRTs have pressure-sensitive screens (*touch screens*) that the user can touch with a finger, telling the system which part of the display has been selected.

Sound

The third communications system is by sound. As in graphic communication, the invention of an output device using sound signals came before the invention of an input device. Much research is being done now on vocal input to a computer, especially for use in space. It would be far easier (and more accurate) for an astronaut to speak commands to a computer than to set all kinds of switches. Some special-purpose machines have been built that are capable of understanding instructions spoken by a human, but they tend to have a small vocabulary (fewer than 100 words).

With the introduction of the *push-button telephone*, it became possible to transmit information to a computer using the keys of the telephone and to get a vocal reply (from a *voice synthesizer*). The depression of a button on a phone keyboard sends a signal in the form of a particular tone. In some areas, these keyboard phones are being used experimentally to help students with their homework. A computer can ask about mathematical problems and get an answer back from the student through the keys; or it can ask questions that have multiple-choice answers.

Computer Memory

The speed of a computer memory is measured by how long it takes the memory device to find a piece of information and make a copy of it. This time may be very short, in the order of one millionth of a second *(microsecond)*. Some memory speed is measured in billionths of a second *(nanoseconds)*. Disks, drums, and tapes may take seconds or thousandths of seconds *(milliseconds)* to find or transfer information. A computer with a 2.5 microsecond memory is able to find a piece of information in 2.5 millionths of a second.

A piece of information in a memory is usually one one of many thousands. Each part of the memory that can contain a single piece of information (called a *word*) has an associated address so that it can be found. This is almost the same as the scheme we use in finding a house in a city. Each house is identified by a street name and a house number—the house address. In the computer, large numbers are used for addresses and the "street name" is omitted. In the same way that a house address tells nothing about who lives in the house, the word address of a piece of information tells nothing about that information.

The memory of a computer is usually made up of thousands of words. Each word is composed of a set of characters (as is a word in the English language). Since a computer memory is made of electronic devices, it is capable of recording only 1's and 0's. These individual parts of a word are known as *bits*. They are digits of a binary numbering system. Sets of bits within a word may be thought of as larger pieces and treated in a special manner. A collection of bits is called a *byte*. Usually, a byte is made up of eight bits, though this is not true for all computers. Memory capacity often is in quantities of bytes—thousands of bytes (*kilobytes* or K bytes), millions of bytes *(megabytes),* or billions of bytes *(gigabytes).*

When the computer system has more than one input/output device, it is possible to program the computer to make the best use of all its abilities through the simultaneous operation of the devices. Since input/output devices each work at different speeds, it is difficult for the central processing unit to keep track of all that is happening at any one time. Thus, the control of input/output devices has been delegated by the central processing unit to smaller special-purpose computers (called

Personal computers are making it possible for many more people than ever before to become familiar with computers. Personal computers may become as common as the television or the dictionary in homes and offices around the world.

channels) that control the devices and allow the central processing unit to do other work. The channels of the computer system make it possible for a computer to be receiving data from several devices, sending data to several devices, and executing a program—all at the same time.

Each input device has a small memory of its own so that it can receive data independently of the work going on in the central processing unit. This small memory is known as a *buffer*. When the data has been read into the buffer, the input device sends a signal to the computer to *interrupt* its present work and move the data from the buffer memory to the computer memory. This move can be done at electronic speed (memory to memory) rather than at the slower speed of a mechanical reader, which must wait as a punched card moves past the read-write mechanism.

Similarly, the central processing unit can send data from its memory to the buffer memory of the output unit and then go on with more work. When the output unit has completed moving the data to paper tape, card, or printed page, an interrupt signal can be sent back to the central processing unit to say, "I've finished that job; I'm ready for some more."

When devices are directly connected to and controlled by the central processing unit, they are said to be *on-line*. If a computer system produces an answer on a set of punched cards (card deck), the programmer or user has to take them to another machine to get a printed translation of the holes in the cards. That second machine—a card interpreter—not being under the control of the central processing unit, is said to be *off-line*. Similarly, machines used in preparation of cards or diskettes for input to a computer (key entry machines) are also off-line.

The *central processing unit* (CPU) of a computer contains the circuits that control the operations of the system and follow the instructions of a program. This unit may be thought of as the "heart" or "brain" of a computer, since without it the machine could not be classified as a true computer. Computers often are compared on the basis of how many instructions can be executed per second. Many are fast enough that the measure is in "*m*illions of *i*nstructions *p*er *s*econd," *MIPS*.

On old computers, the CPU can usually be idenified as the module on which all the lights and switches are mounted. These lights and switches are rarely used by the programmer, but are put there by the manufacturer to help computer engineers and operators diagnose faults with the machine. In newer models, the CPU is diagnosed and tested by computer engineers through the console CRT rather than with panel lights and switches. Like most machines, a computer can fail because of a faulty wire, a bad component, or a poor power supply. Panel lights and switches together with a keyboard input/output unit make up the *console* of the computer, through which the operator and the computer may directly communicate with each other.

Within the CPU of a computer are *registers*—memory units designed to contain special information for the operation of the unit. These registers contain such information as the address of the instruction to be executed next, the instruction being executed, the result of the last calculation, or the time of day. The lights on the console sometimes show the data stored in these registers, and the switches enable the operator to change these values.

Computer Arithmetic

The memory of a computer contains both the instructions of the program to be followed and the data to be used by that program. In general, the data consists of the numbers to be used in the calculations. Since a word of memory is often designed and built before all of the problems to be solved are known, the memory bank cannot be especially designed for each problem. It is not economical to build a memory bank in which the size of each word is different; so the designers make the number of bits in each word of the memory the same. However, the number of digits in each piece of data used is not necessarily the same. In the computer, numbers are either "filled out" (by adding 0's) or "truncated" (cut off) to fit the word size of the memory. Filling out with 0's doesn't make any difference, but the need to truncate can cause problems.

The process of *truncation* is designed so that the most important digits in a number are saved for calculation. For example, we know the distance from the center of Times Square in New York to the Washington Monument in Washington, D.C., to within a fraction of an inch. Yet if you were to drive from Times Square to the Washington Monument, it would be sufficient to know the distance only to the nearest mile and the time taken to the nearest minute to work out your average speed with satisfactory accuracy. Do you really care whether your average speed was 47 or 47.32841 miles an hour?

The *accuracy* with which a measurement is given, such as the average speed of your car, is the freedom from error of that measurement. Accuracy has nothing to do with the number of digits with which a measurement is stated. The *precision* of a measurement is the degree of accuracy.

The precision of a computer is determined by the number of bits used to present a number (the word size of the computer). The accuracy of a computer is measured by the result of a calculation, which in turn may be affected by the truncation necessary to fit the result back into a word of the memory for storage and later reference.

Since the number of bits in a word of the computer's memory is fixed, the set of numbers it is possible to represent is also fixed. Further, since the memory of a computer is made up only of 1's and 0's, it is not possible to have a number that contains either a sign (plus or minus) or a *radix point* (decimal point, in base 10). To overcome this problem, one bit of each word has been set aside to mean the sign of the number. When this particular bit is 0, the number is positive. When the bit is 1, the number is considered negative or less than 0.

The problem of knowing where the radix point is located is solved by one of two methods. In a fixed point system, the radix point is assumed to be either at the left hand end or the right hand end of the number, depending on the particular machine. In a *floating point* system, the word of the memory is divided into two parts, the *exponent* and the *mantissa*. The mantissa is a *fixed-point* number, usually a proper fraction, and the exponent is an integer (whole number) indicating how many places the radix should be moved to put it into its proper position. The exponent also has a special bit indicating whether the radix point should be moved left or right.

Data Organization

The organization of data for the purpose of input or output into *blocks* or groups is a system that speeds up operations. If the work of the central processing unit had to be interrupted every time enough information had been read by the input unit to fill one word of the memory, the efficiency of the system would be reduced. The collection of data into blocks, called *records,* and the ability to store a complete block of data in the input buffer before interrupting the central processing unit allows the system to operate more efficiently. Similarly, if the central processing unit can fill the output unit's buffer with a complete record at its own speed, rather than just one word of data at a time, the central processing unit can perform many more calculations than would be possible if it had to be interrupted every time the output unit was ready to send one word of data.

When records are put on a magnetic tape or disk or are prepared for input on such devices, the collection of records is a *file.* A collection of words is a record, and a collection of records is a file.

Data Processing

The term "data processing" covers all aspects of computing and is not necessarily restricted to computers as we have defined them here. Any processing operation that takes in data and produces more data is a data processing operation. Within this wide classification, there exists the restricted operations of business data processing and scientific processing.

Business data processing usually involves the use of a computer system in information management for a business. The use of a computer by a bank is an example. Any use of a computer to help in the administration of a business, which may include highly scientific calculations (such as financial forecasting or the calculation of the best way to operate an assembly line), may be considered part of business data processing.

Scientific processing is the use of a computer system to solve a problem related to understanding a natural phenomenon or designing an engineering project. The use of computers in the space program to direct and monitor space exploration is an application of scientific processing.

Both scientists and business executives need to get information quickly and accurately. With the large libraries of books and documents available today, it is expensive for scientists to "browse" until they find what they want. It is better for the computer to have this information in its memory and provide it to a scientist on demand. The computer can identify a book of interest far more quickly than a person can look through a library catalog. Even then, the scientist may not want to read the whole book. He or she may be interested only in one subject or one chapter of that book. The library may contain several books on the same topic, and the scientist may not have time to read all the books. In that case, the computer can store summaries and combine all the available information to give a scientist what is needed, by searching the library in far less time than a person could possibly do it.

Similarly, business executives need to have at their fingertips all the current information on their companies and perhaps on their competitors. This, too, could fill a whole library, and this information is changing all the time. A computer can provide the same kind of service to the

Workers can enter data on these key entry machines that may be later used on other computers.

executive as to the scientist. This service is known as *information storage and retrieval.* A collection of stored information that is indexed and easily retrieved is called a *database.*

In both business and scientific operations, it is not always possible to experiment with a process to find out "what would happen if . . ." For example, it would be costly to find out by launching a rocket all the possible things that could go wrong in a space shot to the moon. Instead, the scientist uses a mathematical model of a process and finds out what happens to the model when certain influences (stimuli) are applied to it. This process is known as *simulation.* Simulation also is being used in education to teach students what happens when they make a decision or do something to a process.

Real-Time Processing

Computers are used mainly to solve problems that have no direct effect on what is happening at the time the calculations are being

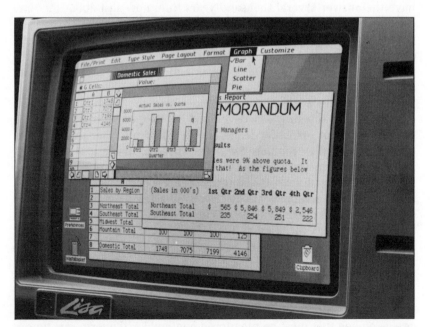

Office automation systems allow a worker to use the computer in the same way he uses his desk. Several tasks can be handled at the same time.

performed. They also are used to control processes, such as the rolling of steel in a mill, the manufacture of paper, or the production of chemicals, which require that calculations be done as the processes go on. This is *real-time processing*. In many cases, computers not only control a process but also monitor the result and then predict what will happen if the current trends continue. In a chemical plant, for example, a computer can control and direct the operations of the plant and also take emergency action to prevent accidents. A human doing the same job could not recognize a problem or react as fast.

Computers used in the space program operate in real time. To do so, it is necessary for the computer to perform calculations at such a speed that it predicts what will happen before it does happen. If the computer were too slow, it would be useless.

Operating in real time, however, is not always fast enough. Astronomers have been trying to discover what happens when a star explodes. They know how to perform the calculations, but computers now are too slow to solve the problem. If they started today, astronomers would have the answer several thousand years from now, just about the time the effects of a star exploding today might reach the earth.

Another aspect of real-time processing, though not as critical, is time sharing. A computer is said to be *time sharing* if it is able to divide its resources (input/output units, storage, and arithmetic abilities) among several users at the same time. Since a computer system can perform input/output jobs at the same time the central processing unit is doing calculations, a scheme was developed so that one program can be performing input or output while another program is being executed. Input/output is slow compared with the speed of the central processing unit; therefore many problems can be solved while one program is waiting for input/output. By combining this scheme with the ability of the computer to communicate by telephone signals, many programmers can be served at once, and the efficiency of the computer is improved by using all of its facilities at the same time. Such systems are now available in most universities and many schools, as well as in most banks.

Time-sharing computer sytems can be considered real-time systems since they provide service on demand. But since the timing of the response to such a demand is not critical (usually about 1 second) and no process is on-line that must be monitored continually, the term real time is reserved for critical systems.

Distributed Processing

Recently, computers have been connected to each other as well as to users through *telecommunications networks.* Connected by these networks, computers are able to share each other's storage and computing power working as a team. They can distribute the work of a large problem among themselves to get the fastest possible response.

When computers work together in this fashion, the activity is called *distributed processing.* An everyday example can be found at a modern supermarket, where each cashier uses a cash register (which is a small computer) connected to a larger computer in the store. The larger computer keeps track of how much each item costs and how many items are on the shelves. When a customer checks out, the cashier— through the cash register—asks the central computer how much the items cost and subtracts the quantity from the central computer's inventory. In this way the central computer knows when stocks are low and can reorder goods even as sales are made during the day.

Computer Installations

Since there are now many thousands of computers in this country, it should not be difficult to find a computer installation within driving distance of your home. Before you go, find out what kind of work it does. Is it business data processing or scientific processing? What kind of machine is it and who is the manufacturer?

A visit to a computer installation can be unrewarding unless you are prepared to ask questions. Don't worry that you might ask silly questions. If possible, follow the steps in which a programmer sets up a job. Start by meeting with a programmer, and see where he or she works. Find out what language is used to communicate with the computer. Ask if you can see a copy of a program. Find out how the program is converted into a form to be read by the computer. Does the computer use cards or magnetic tape? Follow the program through an input/output room to the computer. Be there when the program is run and see the output being produced by the computer.

Get a plan of the computer room, if possible, and mark on it where each component of the computer is placed. Find out how much air conditioning is used, how much electrical power is needed to run the computer, how many people work for the center, who uses it, how much it costs to operate each hour, and all the other questions that you'll think of yourself.

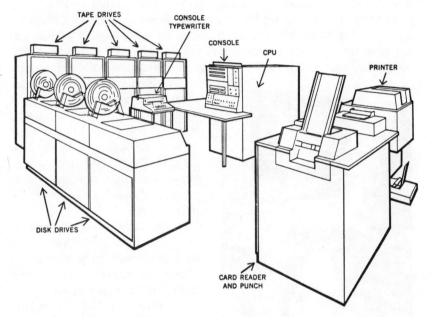

A typical computer installation

Personal Computing

Computers are being used more often in the same way that personal appliances are used at work and at home. In many offices the type-writer is being steadily replaced by small computers that perform *word processing*. The computer keeps track of page numbers and margins, and some can even detect words that may be misspelled. Word processing operators can use a television screen as a kind of electronic blackboard that can arrange and rearrange material much faster than any

Graphs can tell more than numbers sometimes.

typist could possibly work. This pamphlet was prepared using a word processing system. Many large newspapers send all of their material through a computer that gathers the stories and, under human direction, designs, proofs, prints, and bundles the papers for distribution.

In the home, personal computers are used to write letters, set up a household budget, track income and expenses, and keep records such as recipes and phone and mailing lists. They can be programmed to help students with homework. Many people do their own tax accounting, checkbook balancing, and financial planning with the help of personal computers.

Personal Computing Networks

In many communities television viewers can subscribe to cable television systems that offer a wide variety of channels and programs. In some areas these cables also allow subscribers to connect their personal computers to the cable network. Through this network people can buy and sell stocks and bonds, read "mail order" catalogs, and order goods and services directly through their personal computer without leaving the house or making a phone call. Almost all of the applications of computers that we've looked at so far may eventually be available through a personal computer in your own home.

Writing a Program

Go to a local school, library, or computer store and find a beginner's book on programming personal computers. Try to choose a book that describes a programming language available on a computer you can use to try out the program. With the guidance of your counselor, write and run a program.

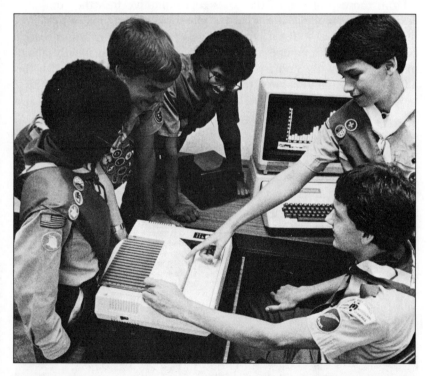

A personal computer similar to the one above may be available for you to run your program. Your counselor will be able to help you find a beginner's book to help you get started.

Careers in the Computer Field

Initially, the *computer sales representative* for a computer manufacturer (who probably already has a number of computer models on the market) contacts his or her clients to find out what their future needs are likely to be. The clients describe what they think their institute or company will be doing in years to come.

From those projections, the sales representative tells the computer company's *design engineer* what the client needs a computer to do. At the same time, the design engineer has been following the research being done by the computer company and knows what new products might be ready. By putting together the needs of the client with the abilities of the manufacturer, the design engineer begins the design of a new computer system. Once the engineer has a rough idea what the

Users, analysts, and programmers work together to develop a good computer system. Teamwork is an important part of careers in the computer field.

new computer will look like, he or she simulates the new machine on an existing computer to find out if the design will work.

Customer engineers are local representatives of the computer manufacturer who install and maintain computers at the customer's place of business. As new computers are designed, customer engineers are trained and readied for the first deliveries. Unlike a car or a toaster, a large computer cannot be sent back to the factory for repairs; the customer engineer must travel to the client. Also, each order for a computer system probably will be different from every other order, because of differing amounts of memory and input/output devices required to suit the exact needs of the client. Since computers are expensive, clients will take only as much equipment as they need. Fortunately, most computers are built so that additional units may be added later as needed.

Before the computer is delivered to the client, the client's *computer operators* have to be trained. Most manufacturers conduct training schools at their plants or offices for the people who will operate a newly delivered computer. Small machines can be operated by relatively inexperienced people after only a day of training, but the operation of larger machines may require several weeks or months to learn.

Since each model of a computer is designed individually, the machine language of the computer will not necessarily be the same as that of another model, though the higher-level languages are expected to be the same on all machines. Thus, *programmers* at the client's place of business also must start training before the machine is installed. In this way, when the machine is ready to start operations, the operators will have been trained to operate it and the programmers will know how to write programs for it. No time is wasted.

Meanwhile, the computer manufacturer's programmers have been developing software for the sytem to translate higher-level languages, to control a time-sharing system, and to supervise the general operation of the system. Without these programs, it would be difficult for the customer's programmers to efficiently use the machine.

Like the computer hardware, the computer software system needs to be maintained during use. Often the manufacturer finds better ways of doing things that will help the customer's programmers, or the company may find that the software contains some errors. It is difficult to return software to the factory for repair, and so a *systems engineer* works with the customer to service the software.

A representative of the company that took delivery of the computer who has a problem and who is not a programmer will go to a computing center for help. Initially, the company's representative meets with a *systems analyst* who will determine what the problem is and whether it can be solved by the computer. If it's decided that the problem will be solved by the computer, the analyst will work with the company's representative to find out in detail how the problem can be solved and what information will be needed for a solution. This is known as systems analysis and design. When all this information is gathered, the analyst and the representative meet with the programmer, whose job it is to translate the analyst's statement of the problem into a program. Once this is done, a test solution is run to find out if the program works as expected to be sure no errors have been made, either in stating the problem or in writing a program for its solution. Finally, when the program has been tested and is running properly, the programmer and the analyst write instructions for how to use the program and give these to the company's representative, who uses the program to solve the problem.

We have discussed the types of jobs that are available both in a manufacturer's plant or office and in the customer's installation center or office. Other opportunities include *data entry operators,* clerical staff, receptionists, report writers, managers, and many others associated with business. Take the opportunity when you visit a computer installation to ask about careers in the computer industry. Ask about the education needed for each job.

From the college or university nearest you, find out what courses are offered that will prepare you for a career in this field. Then find out what courses you will need in high school to satisfy the requirements of college entrance. Your public library and school library have books you can read to help you better understand particular computer uses: computers in space, computers in business and society, computers in medicine, computers in the home. Why not find a beginner's book on programming personal computers and try to write a simple program just to get a feeling for what programming is all about?

Books About Computers

Thanks to the Boy Scouts of America Advisory Committee of the Association for Library Service to Children and to the Children's Services Computer Book Committee of the Cuyahoga County Public Library for the preparation of this bibliography.

Computer Literacy

Ardley, Neil. *Computers*. Watts, 1983.
Ardley describes computers, their parts, programming, history, how they work, and their impact on society.

Berger, Melvin. *Word Processing*. Watts, 1984.
The author defines "word processing" and then describes the various features such as editing, formatting, etc.

Billings, Charlene. *Microchip: Small Wonder*. Dodd, 1984.
Details of how a chip is made and works is illustrated with sharp black-and-white photos. There is also a chapter on the future use and design of the microchip.

Cooper, Carolyn E. *Electronic Bulletin Boards*. Watts, 1985.
Explains how data communication works via computers as well as how to obtain access to on-line usage for individual computers. Organization, term definitions, index, and appendixes are very thorough.

D'Ignazio, Fred. *Electronic Games*. Watts, 1982.
Includes history as well as how the games work, plus a consumer-oriented comparison of various electronic games.

D'Ignazio, Fred. *Messner's Introduction to the Computer*. Messner, 1984.
This introduction relates the evolution of the computer from its pioneer inventors to the development of various computer languages, games, and modern computer applications. It also includes a brief discussion of the future.

D'Ignazio, Fred. *The Science of Artificial Intelligence*. Watts, 1984.
Artificial intelligence is what enables a machine to think like a living creature. Matching human intelligence is a distant goal. The book also explains its use in robot and computer technology.

D'Ignazio, Fred. *The Star Wars Question and Answer Book About Computers*. Random, 1983.
An appealing colorful question-and-answer format uses R2-D2 and C-3PO of *Star Wars* fame to guide the reader through the new technologies of computer applications.

Greene, Laura. *Careers in the Computer Industry*. Watts, 1983.
Business uses, data processing, systems analysis and programming, engineering and technical careers are all described.

Greene, Laura. *Computer Pioneers*. Watts, 1985.
More than 25 early computer pioneers are biographically described from Blaise Pascal in the 1600s to Grace Murray Hopper who helped to develop COBOL in the 20th century.

Herda, D. J. *Computer Maintenance*. Watts, 1985.
The maintenance of computers deals with troubleshooting, dirt and pollutants, heat buildup, electromagnetic interference, static electricity, power disturbances, and mechanical malfunctions.

Hintz, Sandy, and Hintz, Martin. *Computers in Our World, Today and Tomorrow*. Watts, 1983.
Computers in medicine, business, government, law enforcement, science and technology, entertainment, education, and at home are discussed.

Illustrated Computer Dictionary. Childrens Press, 1983.
More than 1,000 terms are briefly defined in this helpful handbook written by the editors of *Consumer Guide*.

Litterick, Ian. *How Computers Work*. Watts, 1984.
In a colorful, appealing format, the computer is presented with focus on its parts, silicon chips, power pack, memory, keyboards, visual and flat displays, etc.

Markle, Sandra. *Kids' Computer Capers*. Morrow, 1983.
Beginning with an exciting computer game scenario, this computer book gives a little history, a little technology, and a little programming.

Richman, Ellen. *The Random House Book of Computer Literacy*. Random, 1984.
This concise presentation of how computers work, their uses, and how to program in BASIC uses many diagrams and cartoons.

Simon, Seymour. *Your First Home Computer*. Crown, 1985.
Using an informal, friendly style, the author discusses how to buy, use, and maintain a personal computer.

Stevens, Lawrence. *Computer Graphics Basics*. Prentice-Hall, 1984.
Techniques of computer graphics on the home computers serve as an art medium tool.

Stwertka, Albert, and Stwertka, Eve. *Computers in Medicine*. Watts, 1984.
Discusses the many ways that computers are used in medicine such as in the admitting department, research through data banks, and in the design and manufacture of artificial limbs and joints.

How to Program

Ault, Rosalie S. *BASIC Programming for Kids*. Houghton Mifflin, 1983.
Ault's guide to programming the home computer in BASIC for Apple, Atari, Commodore, Radio Shack, Texas Instruments, and Timex Sinclair computers emphasizes the ways computers are both fun and helpful.

Boren, Sharon. *A PET for Kids*. Dilithium Press, 1983.
Teaches programming for the Commodore 64 computer, the PET, and VIC-20. It gives an introduction to the keyboard, flow charts, loops, variables, and strings with an emphasis on writing BASIC game programs with graphics.

Galanter, Eugene. *Elementary Programming for Kids in BASIC*. Putnam, 1983.
Introduces and explains the functions of looping, branching, and displays. Educational and game programming exercises, ranging from simple to challenging, are included.

Herriott, John. *Using and Programming the Commodore 64, Including Ready-to-Run Programs*. TAB Books, 1984.
The strengths of this title are the step-by-step explanations and programs and the listing of many demonstration programs. BASIC programming is taught up through arrays, sprites, subroutines, and special tricks.

Lampton, Christopher. *BASIC for Beginners*. Watts, 1984.
Excellent introduction to programming in BASIC builds from simple programs to ones that are complex.

Lampton, Christopher. *Computer Languages*. Watts, 1983.
Brief information on several computer languages is presented here: Assembly, FORTRAN, COBOL, BASIC, Pascal, and LOGO.

Lampton, Christopher. *Programming in BASIC*. Watts, 1983.
BASIC was originally developed as a language for teaching computer programming. Lampton explains how to write both simple and more sophisticated programs.

Markle, Sandra. *The Programmer's Guide to the Galaxy.* Lothrop, 1984.
Galactic adventures provide programming techniques in BASIC with
games, trivia, and puzzles. A glossary and a command conversion table
for the IBM, Apple, Commodore 64, VIC-20, and Timex 1000 are
appended.

Morrill, Harriet. *BASIC Programming for IBM Personal Computers.* Little,
1984.
Beginning with an introduction to IBM commands and working through
possible problems, the text discusses binary codes, BASIC commands
commonly used, and specific features including graphics, animation,
music, and various kinds of data files.

Parker, Pat, and Kennedy, Teresa. *LOGO Fun.* Scholastic, 1985.
A series of easy LOGO programs for the Apple, Atari, or TI computers
includes runs of the resulting graphic patterns.

Ruane, Pat, and Hyman, Jane. *LOGO Activities for the Computer: A Beginner's Guide.* Messner, 1984.
This introduction to programming in LOGO focuses on the graphics use
of the language.

Schneiderman, Ben. *Let's Learn BASIC: A Kid's Introduction to BASIC
Programming on the IBM Personal Computers.* Little, 1984.
This introduces BASIC using stories, riddles, graphics, games, poetry, and
simple computations. (Available also for Atari, Apple, and Commodore
computers.)

Programs for Input

Chance, David. *Twenty-five Exciting Computer Games in BASIC for All
Ages.* TAB Books, 1983.
Presents 25 ready-to-type program games that include a listing, sample
run, flow chart, and short narrative for each one. All are written for the
TRS-80.

Fox, Michael. *Quick 'n Fun Games for the IBM Personal Computer.*
ARCsoft, 1984.
Twenty-five short program games are easy to type and fun to play in
IBM BASIC. Listings and narratives are included.

Heiserman, David. *One Hundred One Programming Surprises and Tricks
for Your Atari Computer.* TAB Books, 1984.
The title means what it says: These 101 programs are not necessarily
all games but are more like puzzles, jokes, and elbow-jabbing tricks. The

listings are short and there are few narrative summaries. Also available for the TRS-80, Commodore 64, Apple II/IIe, and IBM-PC.

Manes, Stephen, and Somerson, Paul. *Computer Olympics.* Scholastic, 1984.
The 39 sports programs are ready to type and are adapted for eight different computers with ample discussion of how to debug a program.

Ramella, Richard. *Computer Carnival.* Green, 1982.
TRS Level II BASIC is the language of these 60 ready-to-be copied programs, listed from the shortest to the longest. Included are word games, codes, tricks, number conundrums, etc.

Speitel, Tom. *Science Computer Programs for Kids . . . and Other People: Apple Version.* Reston, 1984.
Experiment with programs in astronomy, biology, chemistry, hydraulics, mapping, psychology, or waves. A short introduction is followed by the program listing of 10-400 lines. Also available in a Commodore, TI, and VIC-20 computer version.

White, Fred. *Easy Apple Computer Programs.* ARCsoft, 1984.
A sampling of programs for the Apple will accomplish tasks like computing commissions, interests, and percentages. There are also number games, geography quizzes, and the like.

Zuanich, Margaret Ann, and Lipscomb, Susan Drake. *BASIC Fun With Graphics: The Apple Computer Way.* Avon, 1983.
A series of computer graphics listings for the Apple in BASIC includes the programs: Bugs, Christmas Tree, Candy Jar, and Rocket Ship. Other books in the series are similar for the IBM-PC and the Atari.

Index to Subjects and Terms

Acknowledgements

The Boy Scouts of America is grateful to J. A. N. Lee, Ph.D., of Virginia Polytechnic Institute, for his assistance in preparing the original text of the *Computers* merit badge pamphlet, and to Leslie J. Waguespack, Jr., Ph.D., assistant professor of computer science at Louisiana State University, for his assistance as technical and editorial consultant in the preparation of this revised edition. The Boy Scouts of America also is grateful to the Baton Rouge Chapter of the Data Processing Management Association for its assistance in preparing this revised edition and to its Computers merit badge review committee for its assistance in formulating the revised requirements. Members of the committee are David Johnson, chairman; Jim Anderson; Coney Barré; Cecilia Franklin; Marvin Halbrook; Curtis Hatcher; Mary Jordan; Herb Laidlaw; Walt Leonardi; Jim Marquette; and Mike Allen. The Boy Scouts of America also thanks Robert N. Elkins, Region 3 vice-president of the DPMA, for his assistance in coordinating the revision project.

Photo Credits

Lawrence A. Mann, Jr.—Cover, pages 4, 26, 28, 38, 44, 48, 53, 64, and 65.